WORK IS A 4-LETTER WORD

WORK IS A 4-LETTER WORD
Text Copyright 2018 by Richard I. Gold

All rights reserved. No part of this book may be reproduced or transmitted in any form or by any means, electronic or mechanical, including photocopying, recording, or by any information storage and retrieval system without written permission from the publisher or the author. The only exception is brief quotations for reviews.

For information address:

J2B Publishing LLC
4251 Columbia Park Road
Pomfret, MD 20675
www.J2BLLC.com
GladToDoIt@gmail.com

Printed and bound in the United States of America

ISBN: 978-1-94E8747-19-6

WORK IS A 4-LETTER WORD

Richard I. Gold

Also by Richard I. Gold

God's Agenda - Religious Poems - Vol. I
Mary's Lamb and other Christmas Poems
God's Love - Easter Poems
Sayings for the Believer
God's Love – Easter Poems

DEDICATION

My thanks to my wife, Penny Gold, who assisted me as I wrote these poems and compiled these ideas. I also wish to thank Jim Greenlee and Ms. Betty Rehberg who reviewed the printed version and made suggested improvements.

BACKGROUND

Much of our life in this civilization is concerned with the work we do to support our family and our desires. This listing of statements about work and original poems has several ideas which may contain applications for our every day existence.

TABLE OF CONTENTS

This book contains 2 parts. The first part is a list of statements about work, one for each day of the year (366) which the author has observed from his work experience. The reader will have had a different experience and may find that some of the statements may not fit their own present experience.

The second part is a list of poems which may cover the same topic but has poems which apply to other parts of their working life.

STATEMENTS ABOUT WORK - - - - - 5

JANUARY - 6
FEBRUARY - 9
MARCH - 12
APRIL -15
MAY -18
JUNE -21
JULY - 24
AUGUST - 27
SEPTEMBER - 30
OCTOBER - 33
NOVEMBER -36
DECEMBER - 39

POEMS ABOUT WORK - - - - - - - - - - - - - - - - - 42

1. WORK IS A 4-LETTER WORD - - - - - - - - - - - - - - 43
2. A DAY AT WORK - 44
3. MONEY - 45
4. THE MONEY IN THE SKY - - - - - - - - - - - - - - - - -46
5. DELEGATION -47
6. WHEN YOU BUY -48
7. IT'S EASY TO RUN UP DEBT - - - - - - - - - - - - - - 49
8. TQL/TQM - 50
9. TQL -51
10. WORK - 52
11. WORK IS THE FATE - - - - - - - - - - - - - - - - - - 53
12. WORK IS THE FATE OF MAN - - - - - - - - - - - - - 54
13. WORK, WORK, WORK - - - - - - - - - - - - - - - - - 55
14. YOU GO TO WORK - - - - - - - - - - - - - - - - - - - 56
15. WE WORK FOR OTHERS - - - - - - - - - - - - - - - 57
16. WE WORK - 58
17. THE NEW EMPLOYEE - - - - - - - - - - - - - - - - - 59
18. TAKE A JOB - 60
19. TAKE THIS JOB - 61
20. LOOKING FOR A JOB - - - - - - - - - - - - - - - - - -62
21. SLEEPING ON THE JOB - - - - - - - - - - - - - - - - 63
22. WHEN SITTING IN A MEETING - - - - - - - - - - - - 64
23. WHEN IN A MEETING - - - - - - - - - - - - - - - - - - 65
24. MEETINGS - 66
25. THE SPECIAL SPOT - - - - - - - - - - - - - - - - - - -67
26. THE INTERVIEW - 68
27. THE INTERNET - 69
28. THE PRESENTATION - - - - - - - - - - - - - - - - - -70
29. THE SPEAKER -71
30. THE LECTURER - 72
31. THE CONTRACTOR - - - - - - - - - - - - - - - - - - -73

32. ATTENTION SPAN - 74
33. THE SPONSOR - 75
34. EVERYTHING HAS A PRICE - - - - - - - - - - - - - - 76
35. SYSTEM ENGINEERING - - - - - - - - - - - - - - - - - --77
36. THE DENTIST --79
37. THE DOCTOR - 80
38. MODERN TECHNOLOGIES - - - - - - - - - - - - - - - - 81
39. WHAT WILL YOU DO - - - - - - - - - - - - - - - - - - -82
40. WE WALK A FINE LINE - - - - - - - - - - - - - - - - - -83
41. THE WORLD HAS BEEN HERE - - - - - - - - - - - - - -84
42. THE CHALLENGES WE FACE - - - - - - - - - - - - - - -85
43. THE RESTAURANT -86
44. WHO IS THE EXPERT? - - - - - - - - - - - - - - - - - -87
45. WHAT A PERSON HAS - - - - - - - - - - - - - - - - - - 88
46. WHEN WE WENT TO SCHOOL - - - - - - - - - - - - -89
47. VOLUNTEER - 90
48. WE WORK -- 91
49. WE ARE ALL OCCUPIED - - - - - - - - - - - - - - - - -92
50. SUCCESS - 93
51. AWARDS -94
52. A PROJECT -95
53. THE BUDGET PROCESS - - - - - - - - - - - - - - - - - -96
54. BUDGET TIME -97
55. BUDGET DAY - 98
56. THE MORNING GREETING - - - - - - - - - - - - - - - - 99
57. BOOM YEARS -100
58. MAKE A DIFFERENCE - - - - - - - - - - - - - - - - - -101
59. TECHNOLOGY IS GROWING - - - - - - - - - - - - - - --102
60. THE INSPECTIONS -103
61. DECISIONS - 104

STATEMENTS ABOUT WORK

As humans, we make a living in many ways. We refer to the effort we expend as work. The effort a person works at can be, and should be, a source of pride in an effort performed and a result achieved.

No effort that is work, whether physical or mental, is more important than any other unless the one doing it does not do a good job with a good effort. The farmer in the field is important in the production of food. The laborer in the factory is important in the production of a product that others use. The office worker is important in the flow and organization of physical work and other office work. The supervisor is important to provide the resources to get the job done and to direct the effort with the fewest conflicts and to determine when the job is complete.

Be proud of your effort and the product or service that you do.

JANUARY

1. Work is the way we make a living.

2. Work is a four letter word.

3. Always expand your knowledge of your job.

4. We must work to live.

5. Everything that is important to anyone represents an expenditure of time and effort.

6. Time is all we have.   Time and effort is what we have to sell to our employer.

7. Everyone is an employee of someone else.

8. Knowledge makes work more valuable.

9. Always try to give more to your employer than you receive.

10. Employers must realize that healthy, content employees are their most valuable asset.

11. An employee who robs their employer is no better than the employer who robs their employees.

12. Work is a commitment of your time.
13. Work can be a positive experience.

14. We meet interesting people at work.

JANUARY

15. Morning is the most productive time of day.

16. People who do not know their job cannot advance.

17. Be a most valuable employee.

18. The first job a person has generally not the only one they will have.

19. We can only do the job if we have the tools.

20. For humans work produces wealth.

21. The better paying your job is, the better you are treated.

22. The company that demands loyalty from its employees must give loyalty in return.

23. During times of labor peace everyone can profit, during times of labor unrest everyone loses.

24. When labor will not work nothing gets done.

25. The stockholder is gambling on the wisdom of the management and the ability of the employees.

26. Both labor and management must respect the environment.

JANUARY

27. Companies compete with each other to produce a better, more useful product.

28. It is easy for any bureaucracy to become top heavy.

29. Companies that will not change when conditions change are headed for bankruptcy.

30. The best condition is when both management and labor work together for the good of all.

31. When you know something that someone wants, they will pay you to use that knowledge.

FEBRUARY

1. Know how to do your job.

2. Management should never forget their workers are people.

3. All good managers could become good workers but not all good workers could become good managers.

4. Labor is the raw material of production, management is the shaping, and wealth is the product.

5. Learn all you can about your job.

6. Never let your job limit your horizons.

7. Never confuse money with wealth.

8. Those who wish to share the wealth generally don't have any, and if they do, they do not wish to share theirs.

9. Labor should be given a fair wage.

10. Any honest job is better than starving.

11. Work can be an end in itself.

12. Working with things is easier than working with people.

13. No society can exist where the citizens will not work.

FEBRUARY

14. Productive work may be easy or hard, but it is very important.

15. Important jobs are those we often look down on, such as trash collectors, but they support society. If you don't believe it is so, let them all stop.

16. Companies and societies where everyone gives 110% are very successful.

17. The wealth of society is the sum of the effort of the individuals.

18. Society must realize that a healthy population is the raw material of a dynamic, growing economy.

19. Work that we do not like is boring.

20. People begin their working life at the bottom and move up from there.

21. People value their time differently depending upon what they are doing.

22. Work is the product of human effort.

23. Work until you get a job you feel honored to have.

24. Equal pay for equal work and equal work for equal pay.

25. We plan for the best, but our work determines how we advance.

FEBRUARY

26. The most important thing about work is what we put into it, not what we get out of it.

27. People measure our existence in terms of what we do.

28. It is said that "All men are created equal." it is when we compete fairly at work.

29. Your job: love it or leave it.

MARCH

1. The work place can be a place where we purify our souls.

2. Those who have never worked full time cannot know its pleasure.

3. You have to spend your time doing something. It might as well be productive work.

4. We all should be nice to the one who cooks our food.

5. Society is the sum of the individuals. The wealth of society is the sum of their wealth.

6. People who think that life owes them a living will think that life has not paid them enough.

7. The social contract requires everyone that can work will work.

8. The boss should know enough about the job to know if you are doing a good job.

9. If you have a job, hold on to it as long as you need it.

10. People in authority have responsibility.

11. Work smarter not harder.

MARCH

12. There are usually at least three ways to do a job: the hard way, the smart way or sometimes the company way.

13. Sometimes it is good to work for the experience.

14. A family, like a business, depends upon the members to make it successful.

15. The most profound thought about work is that it is.

16. Your boss is looking for someone who knows the answer to their problems.

17. The poor person may envy the rich. The rich person probably works harder and longer than the poor person.

18. You can't afford to get mad at the boss.

19. The customer is king.

20. Companies are set up by bureaucracies.

21. Never begrudge the problems you have on the job. It is the solution of these problems that keeps you employed.

22. A good employee recognizes that they work for themselves.

23. Life is a struggle.

MARCH

24. People who die with many things but no friendships fail.

25. Know this: you must work.

26. Always struggle to move up.

27. The person who loves their job never works.

28. Those who will not work shall not eat.

29. An employee should put in an honest day's work for an honest day's pay.

30. Never underestimate the power of a dedicated person.

31. Never steal from your employer, not even a pencil.

APRIL

1. Learn new knowledge in your job.

2. The customer the final inspector of your work.

3. You're paying job is only one component of your life.

4. A good boss is a blessing. A bad boss is a curse.

5. A friend from work may become a personal friend, or maybe not.

6. People respect power, even at work.

7. To be a success in business, learn from your mistakes. Try not to make them the first time.

8. Sometimes our avocation becomes our vocation.

9. Those who have responsibility have authority and those who have authority have responsibility.

10. Never confuse what you want with company goals.

11. Never confuse professional friendships with personal friendships.

12. Education is a shortcut to experience. Experience makes a worker valuable.

APRIL

13. Know that your job is an important part of your life. Choose your profession wisely.

14. At the beginning of a new job there is much to learn.

15. Never be too friendly with the boss.

16. What do you want from life?   You will have to work to get what you want.

17. Never mix anything with work.   Not love, not gambling, not anything.

18. The work place can be very lonely.

19. The employee has an obligation to their employer; the employer has an obligation to their employees.

20. When you are young you can't wait to retire.   When you are old you don't want to.

21. It is the duty of employers to deal fairly with their employees.

22. Bosses should defend those who work for them.

APRIL

23. You cannot expect to get a job for which you are not qualified.

24. A child needs to be taught to work. Most of the time they don't like the lesson, but in life this is one of the most important lessons.

25. Your boss will not teach you to spell.

26. The best boss is competent.

27. Good health care is in the company's interest.

28. The worker who despises their job should look for another.

29. Honor all you hold dear with your effort.

30. The measure of our worth to society is what we give, not what we get.

MAY

1. Bosses do not like surprises.

2. You can get ahead by making your boss look good.

3. Any job can be a good job if we know how to work it.

4. There are more jobs at the bottom than at the top.

5. A boss should be a good leader.

6. If you do not understand what your boss wants you to do, ask.

7. The end of a job should be as sweet as the beginning.

8. You should always respect your boss.

9. One person's work can be another person's pleasure.

10. People are made to work. It is the way we all are happy.

11. The most miserable person is the one who has nothing to do.

12. The child's play is their work.

13. Work is a good way to pass the time.

14. If you would be known, be the best you can be.

MAY

15. When you lose a job you can learn from your mistakes.

16. Very few people always do the right thing.

17. Work is the fate of all people.

18. Never be glad when a fellow employee is put down. You may be next.

19. No company can exist when the workers will not work.

20. We all make mistakes: most of them are recoverable.

21. At first a job is a job for the pay. Later it becomes a position with a salary.

22. Management is the one responsible for what the workers do.

23. The boss wants the same ends as the employee.

24. It is the duty of children who are offered an education to do their best.

25. Honor those who work.

26. In the spring it is easy to think about things other than work.

MAY

27. The work that you do is important to someone.

28. Always try to work your way up in your job.

29. An employee of a big company can get lost in the shuffle. An employee in a small company can have too much attention on their performance.

30. The boss's child has a vested interest in the company that you can never have.

31. An employee should never ask to be paid more than they are worth.   An employer should always pay their employees what they are worth.

JUNE

1. Never despise your job. Keep it until you get something better.

2. All honest work is honorable.

3. No person owns a job and no job owns a person.

4. Some people never like the boss.

5. The boss should never talk down about the company.

6. It is the job of the boss to get the job done.

7. No person can work two full-time jobs and perform them both well.

8. A job is a possession. Strive to keep it as long as you need it.

9. The social contract is one that requires the best from all of us.

10. Never blame others for your failures.

11. There is always a better way to do any task.

12. The owner of the business has the right to hire and fire.

JUNE

13. No one has the right to destroy the company they work for.

14. Jobs are the first thing cut in a recession and the last thing created in a recovery.

15. Very few people work the same job all their life.

16. The government can mandate what it will. It must know that all additional requirements cost money. Some may not produce income to offset their cost. These may cost business their existence.

17. Human effort is the yardstick by which we measure the worth of things.

18. Human effort generates wealth.

19. Bosses should realize that their future depends upon their employees.

20. In America the worker can become a stockholder and even the owner.

21. We work until we retire, then we really get busy.

22. Before you enter the work force you must be trained. As you leave the work force you may train others.

JUNE

23. At all times, people have had to work for a living.

24. There are no unimportant jobs.

25. Without human effort there can be no wealth.

26. Never forget who pays you.

27. There is a joy in a good day's work well done.

28. Children learn to work by watching their parents.

29. Work is the task set for us.

30. The amount of money you make generally goes up. The price of things you can buy may not.

JULY

1. It is good to come home after a hard day's work.

2. It is the prerogative of management to set policy. It is the duty of the employees to follow that policy. If there is a disagreement, there should be a means to talk about it.

3. Begin your day by planning what you are going to do.

4. No employer wants an employee who steals from them.

5. Never trust a boss who has things other than business on their mind.

6. Employers want workers to be dedicated to getting the job done well.

7. We all sacrifice something for our jobs.

8. Everyone wants to be rich. Only the few make it.

9. Retirement is the end of one career and the beginning of another.

10. Love your work the best way you can.

11. Never be put in a position of having to justify your existence.

12. Every person who works should work the best they can.

JULY

13. Even the most satisfying job has its drudgery.

14. A rising tide lifts all boats and a sinking tide lowers all boats.

15. Remember this – We work for the ends we want.

16. The success of all societies depends upon the individual.

17. Those who work hard generally play hard.

18. It is a sin to overwork children.

19. People have many jobs, not just the one that pays the bills.

20. Employers hire you to get the job done.

21. Some professions are overpaid.

22. Never let yourself be fired.

23. Retirement is a time to think much, speak some and do what you want.

24. There are some modes of dress that are not appropriate for work.

25. You are the inspiration to another.

JULY

26. The boss is responsible for your performance.

27. Always strive to perform well enough to take your boss's job.

28. You define your life in terms of what you do.

29. Not everyone who is looking for a job can do it.

30. Every person has dreams about their job.

31. Ask yourself if you would pay yourself what the boss pays you for what you do.

AUGUST

1. No person is above the need to work.

2. Taskmasters can be hard.   Our hardest taskmaster can be our self.

3. No one knows your job better than you.

4. Volunteer work for a good cause is the cornerstone of our country.

5. Education is a tool that we can use to get a job.

6. By your work you make yourself valuable to your employer.

7. The volunteer profession is the one we should enjoy doing.

8. Be trustworthy to your boss and to those whom you supervise.

9. The idea of employer responsibility is still valid.

10. If work is drudgery, being out of work is worse.

11. Some people despise their jobs.   They are foolish.

12. Never be content with your present job.   Always try to work your way up.

AUGUST

13. Even the worst job can be made into a good job if you try.

14. If the job is beneath you, do it well and you will move up.

15. Idle hands are the devil's workshop.

16. Retirement is a time to enjoy the fruits of your labor.

17. For some, work is an end in itself.

18. Our work is our life. Our life is our work. When our life ends, so does our work.

19. One of the laws of human existence is that in order to be satisfied a person must be productive.

20. If you want to look for a job, don't quit the job you have until you have a new one.

21. The company does not pay you to do what you want.

22. Do at least enough work to support the organization.

23. No one is indispensable.

24. Plan your work and work your plan.

AUGUST

25. No person has enough of this world's goods to ignore their responsibility to the community.

26. Work your job.   Your job supports you.

27. Advice about the profession a young person should go into is most important.

28. During an economic downturn pay is the first thing to go down and the last thing to go up.

29. Honor your teachers.

30. When you work remember that you have a job to do.

31. Your boss may not always be right; but they are always your boss.

SEPTEMBER

1. A workman should be worth their pay.

2. At work your supervisor sets the goals.

3. Even the lazy worker can turn out a good project.

4. The most difficult task is the one you do not understand. The next most difficult task is the one you do not wish to do.

5. Different societies measure wealth different ways. They all agree that the more wealth a person has the better.

6. To a child, the father and/or mother going to work is inconceivable.

7. Experience is the best teacher.

8. If you lose your job, look upon it as an opportunity to advance.

9. The boss doesn't always know the answer. That is the reason they have employees.

10. Follow the lead of your company.

11. Never give up.

12. Always be flexible.

SEPTEMBER

13. The difference between a recession and a depression is who loses a job. In a recession your neighbor loses their job. In a depression you lose your job.

14. Always be thankful you have a job.

15. Know your limitations. Work up to your limitations.

16. Work is an honorable pastime.

17. To the laborer in the field, it seems that the writer does not work. This is because they have never tried it.

18. No one can make enough money in their lifetime to properly retire.

19. If you make a mistake on the job, learn from it.

20. For the child schooling is their job.

21. Know what it is you want from life.

22. In work, as in every other phase of life, we need role models.

23. Always give more to your job than you get out of it.

24. If a company wants loyalty they must give it.

SEPTEMBER

25. The boss is a person just like you are.

26. Even top management needs a rest now and then.

27. Sometimes the job requires extra effort.   If it does, do it.

28. Everyone can make a contribution to the project.

29. Drink is the curse of the working person.

30. Each job can be challenging if we know how to look at it.

OCTOBER

1. Never try the patience of your fellow workers.

2. Trust on the job is very important.

3. Be forthright with your boss.

4. Always be honest with your boss.

5. Anyone who performs a useful service to the community should be honored.

6. The best way to get fired is to be hard to supervise.

7. Many people do not like their jobs. However, it is better than no job.

8. Some people think of the boss as the enemy. Never let it be so for you.

9. Some companies hire people, some want to own them.

10. You work for your employer, but you are not owned.

11. When it comes to people there is a difference between providing the raw material for an industrialized society and being expendable.

12. Everyone answers to someone.

OCTOBER

13. Management is responsible for providing a safe working environment.

14. The good worker is of value to the company.

15. Never attempt to go into business in competition with your employer.

16. Those who cannot work should not work. Those who can work should.

17. We must be able to trust our employers.

18. The good worker is always busy. The smart worker is always learning.

19. The young must learn how to work. The old must learn how to retire.

20. The happiest job situation is when management and labor have the same goals and work together. The worse job situation is when management and labor have opposite goals and become enemies.

21. Government employees are just like employees in any other industry.

22. We are all bound by regulations.

OCTOBER

23. Never abuse those who work for you.

24. Always be nice to everyone, you can never tell who will someday be your boss or your customer.

25. The young may think that working is a bore. Work bores boring people.

26. There are times when the company cannot keep its promises.

27. When many people are losing their job and you lose yours it is not a bad spot on your record.

28. No company can long exist without profits.

29. Workers should insure that they work safely.

30. Most professions are honorable.

31. Even the laziest person can amount to something.

NOVEMBER

1. Your employer hires you for the skills you have. They pay you for exercising those skills.

2. A good worker is hard to find.

3. It is in the best interest of the company for workers to continue to learn.

4. The skilled worker is the cornerstone of the industrial world.

5. Some jobs never end. Some never begin.

6. Is your work boring? Try to do it better. Find a way to make a game of it.

7. The people who manage are responsible for those they supervise.

8. Work may be a bad way to earn a living, but it is better than no work.

9. Work begins as an opportunity to earn a living and progresses until it is a part of you.

10. No employee is more important than the management.

11. The higher in the corporate ladder you go the greater are the rewards.

NOVEMBER

12. The security of company secrets is in the hands of the employees.

13. We should be grateful that we can work.

14. As we work we may have excess that is trash. The smart company learns to recycle, for a profit.

15. To the laborer the idea of work is repulsive. To the professional, the idea of work is attractive. Some laborers are professional in outlook. Some professionals are laborers in outlook.

16. Understand the company's position. Hope that they understand yours.

17. Work is a human pastime.

18. Work is the only way to achieve our goals.

19. Every successful person is able to sell themselves.

20. The profession of a person is their security.

21. No one person can replace a group in performing a task no matter how good they are.

22. The successful worker has a pride all their own.

NOVEMBER

23. The time spent at work is the majority of our waking lives.

24. A good job is a friend that takes care of you.

25. If you wish to be remembered as a good worker, do your best all of the time.

26. When at work keep busy doing something productive.

27. The fortunate few always have a job they enjoy.

28. The average boss directs. The smart boss plans. The wise boss leads.

29. The lazy person may make a good boss.

30. Hire good people and trust them.

DECEMBER

1. When weather gets cold it is nice to have a warm home.

2. Ill health can cost us more than money.

3. There is a contract (though it may be unwritten) between the worker and the employer.

4. There is something special about coming home after a hard day's work and thinking back on all you have accomplished.

5. Nobody outgrows the need to master the fundamentals.

6. The song says "Take this job and shove it." The reality says "Take this job and love it."

7. An unsafe work place can cost the company more than lost time from the employee.

8. Find out what the job requires before taking it. If you cannot do it, don't take it.

9. Never stay too long at the same job.

10. Work is the way the working person defines themselves.

11. There is never a bad pay day.

12. There is a social contract between the company and the employees. The foolish parties do not recognize this.

DECEMBER

13. Never try to second guess the boss.

14. Give your company a Christmas present. Do a good job.

15. Yesterday was the time to plan. Today is the time for action. Tomorrow will be the time to remember.

16. You may take a job for money. You keep it for satisfaction.

17. The person said "I was looking for a job when I came here. I can look for a job now."

18. The most boring prospect is having nothing to do.

19. The company with a secure work force and a secure market cannot be stopped.

20. Being good at what you do can be a job.

21. The person who wants to rule others must first rule themself.

22. People are designed to work.

23. Monetary rewards come from hard, efficient work and from recognition from the boss.

24. Work can be a very personal thing.

DECEMBER

25. Even Santa Claus has to work.

26. There is no such thing as a free lunch.

27. Holidays should be times of enjoyment and growth.

28. One difference between a bad worker and a good worker is effort.

29. A good worker does not blame their tools.

30. Even the coldest day is better when you have a warm home.

31. In the final analysis, work is worthwhile.

PART II
POEMS ABOUT WORK AND LIFE

1 WORK IS A 4-LETTER WORD

Work is a 4-letter word
And that is not new
We spend our lives at it
It gives us something to do

When we have enough time
Or enough money saved
We set out for retired life
And say that we had slaved

Retirement life is new
A real change in what we do
We start at the beginning
Hope that the end is true

But in the end
It is useful that we must be
For if we are not useful
The future we may not see

2 A DAY AT WORK

A day at work
Another day in life
Solving problems
Cooling strife

Work hard at your job
Work with all your might
If you produce enough
Your boss will see the light

Work is the fate of men
And of women too
That we may live here
It is what we must do

3 MONEY

Money
Like many things in life
Sets us going
It gets us what we want
Keeps our age growing

But money is a fragile thing
With which to measure wealth
It can give us worries
Can cost us our health

Come inflation
When a dollar is worth a dime
When all our savings
Are not worth the time

As long as we can make ends meet
And keep a roof over your head
Be happy and help others
The future we shall not dread

4 THE MONEY IN THE SKY

Every week they have the lotto
Money beyond belief
You can't win if you don't play
It's worse than a thief

Pay your money and take a chance
It'd be so nice to win
But with all that money
It'd be hard not to sin

As long as you make ends meet
Keep a roof over your head
Be happy and help others
The future you shall not dread

5 DELEGATION

Everyone has a job to do
Tasks that must be done
Many details to cover
A program to run

The bottom line is results
In the least money and time
Consistent with quality
The goal is prime

Often there are many tasks
More than anyone can do
So parts must be delegated
To get results, it is true

So if you have many tasks
You must assign some part
And trust someone else
To work it with hart

6 WHEN YOU BUY

When merchandise you buy
You see what is there
But before you pay your money
Remember "Buyer, beware"

Most merchants are honest
Their customers they would not cheat
But always be careful
When a deal seems hard to beat

For you and your money
Have a love affair
Once it has gone
It never will be there

7 IT'S EASY TO RUN UP DEBT

It's easy to run up debt
As easy as living
But when the bills come due
Your creditors will not be forgiving

You make a list
A list headed by "I want"
Before you BUY what's on the list
Consider and don't

Some debts are for money
Some are for time
All debts you must pay interest
Far above the prime

Borrowing is easy
And spending is fun
Repaying is the pits
A rough race to run

Don't take on debts of another
Settle those you own
For how you pay your debts
Will follow you home

8 TQL/TQM

TQL - Total Quality Leadership
TQM - Total Quality Management
This is what the leaders think they want
They send people to class
Some come back, but quality they don't

The watch word for today
Is a word of utility
A word to which we strive
That word is quality

Everything takes time
Effort and money too
We measure the value of something
By the effort it takes to do

But doing something is one thing
Quality of it is important too
For if it breaks before its time
It will require a redo

9 TQL

TQL, TQL, TQL
To go forward
You must ring the bell

Quality Management System
Is what you must establish
If you do not do this
Your job will be abolished

Total quality leadership
Is what the boss desires
For when it comes to being the boss
It is what their boss requires

10 WORK

Work is the fate of men
Who live on this earth
To our dying day
From our day of birth

We prepare and we do
For others, not ourselves
If we our selfish will desire
We will find ourselves on the shelf

The end of man comes all too soon
We will lie in the grave
Those who remember us
Will remember what we gave

11 WORK IS THE FATE

Work is the fate of men
And of woman too
It keeps us out of trouble
And gives us something to do

We do not work solely for gain
Although this is a goal
But for the scarification of work
Which is what we hold

To be useful to others
Is one's chief desire
But when we are used
The consequences dire

So, my son, go forth and work
From sun to setting sun
That when your life is over
You will have some good things done.

12 WORK IS THE FATE OF MAN

Work is the fate of man
And of woman too
So much to accomplish
So little time to do

What is it you'd like to do
To sit and vegetate
Be careful what you do
You may be tempting fate

Work can be a bane
Or yet a blessing too
For sitting home and doing nothing
Will make time go so slow

So work at your job
Do the best you can
You will have laurels
When your race is ran

13 WORK, WORK, WORK

Work, work, work
We all work for others
Even if we're self employed
We cannot do our druthers

Work is the fate of men
Men and women too
The product of mind and hand
Is what we ever do

Reward is the result of work
Doing what others would have
For what they do value
Is the reward for which they live

14 YOU GO TO WORK

You go to work
The same old way
That you've done
Day after day after day

Suddenly you notice things
That has always been there
But they seem different
As thought change is in the air

You see the house
Where people live
Each with their own
Each has much to give

You see the trees
Notice where one's been removed
Looks so different
Your vision is improved

So look around
See the face of man
For these are the ones
For which your life must be run

15 WE WORK FOR OTHERS

We often work for others
Without any pay
We wish to help out
Aid them every day

We do it for the pay they give
It is not in money but in words true
That by their life, and by their hope
They just say "Thank you"

"Thank you" means so much
It really shows they care
Helps us when we sacrifice
To go and be there

16 WE WORK

We all work in life
Work is what we do
We oft define ourselves
By the work is true

When we work
Our employers set the goal
If we are good workers
We follow their lead so bold

There is doing what we want
In that case we set the run
There is wanting to do
Which makes the work more fun

Although they are not the same
The second is oft the better
For it defines our life
Makes it not so bitter

17 THE NEW EMPLOYEE

We've all been there
The first day at work
Who will help us?
Who will be a jerk?

What is expected?
For us to do
What is old hat?
What will be new?

Then we find our desk
A place to call our own
Some place to put our pencils
Occasionally call home

A job is an opportunity
Don't expect anything else
For when we go to work
We work for ourselves

18 TAKE A JOB

You take a job
To earn some doe
You work real hard
Try to make a go

Time passes by
Your family does grow
You do your best
You're in the know

Then one day
Retirement draws near
Your job, your precious job
You suddenly hold dear

You know you must go
You know this is the end
Your retirement life
Is about to begin

19 TAKE THIS JOB

"Take this job and shove it"
Is the message of a song
Quitting is an option
But won't be for long

With an attitude like that
You'll have this job not long
Your means of support
Gone with the song

"Take this job and love it"
Build up the place of work
Make it more that it is
Your duty is "You shall not shirk"

Rewards may come to others
For work that you do
But at the end of the day
Your hard work is for you

20 LOOKING FOR A JOB

You look for a job
To pay the bills
One that's interesting
With a little thrills

You write a résumé
To show what you can do
You might stretch the facts
But don't say what's untrue

Untruth will find you out
Thought hidden in the dark
Shout from the roof tops
All mankind will hark

Then comes the interview
Is this where you wish to work
Do they need you to do the job?
Your duty, you cannot shirk

The job you get to pay the bills
Is something to do you can
You know how to do the work
Training was in your plan

So grow in your job
To be all that you can be
A bright and happy future
Is what you will truly see

21 SLEEPING ON THE JOB

Sleeping is a part of life
An important part of the day
There's a time and place for it
But there are places it doesn't pay

The job at which we work
At which we spend our time
Is the goal of our life
Part of our prime

Sleeping on the job
Is neither good nor right
If you fall asleep
You might lose your job, you might

22 WHEN SITTING IN A MEETING

When setting in a meeting
Sleep sneaks up on you
You would not, should not
You know this is true

Pay attention to what is said
It's repercussions on you will fall
If you should fall asleep
You cannot get on at all

So if you would be known
As one who can pass the test
When night has come
Be sure to get some rest

But if you should fall asleep
Because of the subject matter
Be sure that later on
The speaker to flatter

23 WHEN IN A MEETING

When in a meeting
Listen to what is said
Sometime there are minutes
Written to be read

Often what is written
Is not what was meant
There are other messages
Both received and sent

What is not said?
What is not meant?
Will relay the message
The true intent

24 MEETINGS

Meetings are a fact of life
We often cannot escape
We are drawn into their orbs
Over a chair we drape

Those who run the meetings
Have agendas of their own
We sit and we listen
Weary to the bone

Some meetings are long and dull
They can often be a bore
But ere you fall asleep
Be careful not to snore

25 THE SPECIAL SPOT

A special spot
On the hot plate
Under the spot light
Writing on a slate

The questions are arcane
What relation to the job
Designed for self esteem
To take and rob

The interviewer wishes to know
The depth of your soul
Within his grubby hands
In a straight jacket hold

After it is over
The questions are done
It makes the interviewee wish
To cut and run

26 THE INTERVIEW

The interview for a job
Is a foot in the door
It gives you a chance to sell yourself
That is your chief chore

If you are to be employed
And get the really good job
You have to look your best
Don't be a slob

27 THE INTERNET

The internet can send out mail
At once to all your friends
It gives a way to keep in touch
To use for good ends

Use it for the proper use
Do not bend the mind
For it will help you with your hope
But do not cross the line

When you text a message you should remember
What is there said
Is forever there
Be careful for there is price that must be paid

28 THE PRESENTATION

The room is dark
The projector on
The crowd is hostile
I wish I were home

One in the crowd
Goes to sleep
It is my job
Their attention to keep

View graph after view graph
I've shown
Their disinterest
Has grown

Now the lights come on
The time is over
Will I come back?
The operative word is never

29 THE SPEAKER

I've come to tell you
The speaker said
The future of our life
So don't be in dread

The future will be beautiful
Or so very, very dark
It may be hard and dreary
Or it may be a lark

The future may be hard
Or it may be true
The shape of the future
All depends on you

30 THE LECTURER

The guest lecturer stood so upright and proud
He talked to the students in a voice so loud
His talk of economics was so technical and deep
The students were puzzled and almost put to sleep

Finally the professor interrupted to explain
What the great lecturer had said to all
"If your out-go exceeds your income
Your upkeep will be your down fall."

31 THE CONTRACTOR

The contractor came in
And told us how
They would solve all our problems
They could begin now

But as they talked
Promised us the sky
We finally thought to ask
The central question - "Why?"

32 ATTENTION SPAN

The attention span of a child is short
That of an adult also
To teach them a fact
The presentation must make their interest glow

So when you would teach them a thing
Prepare what you will say
You must be brief, concise and short
To get your message all the way

Make it short
Make it sweet
Your message must be concise
And oh so neat

If you would be remembered
For what you have thought
Your ideas must be in a story
Something they have bought

33 THE SPONSOR

Sponsors are beautiful people
In many, many ways
They bring you support
For your work pays

They help you do your work
So you can support what you have
To live in this world
Have something to give

Sponsors can be a pain
They care about results
When you have problems
It is just your bane

But sponsors are a necessary
For projects both great and small
If you lose your sponsor
You've dropped the ball

34 EVERYTHING HAS A PRICE

As we go through life
We often interact
With other people
This is a fact

When we interact
When they do us good
We owe them something
We must repay
We know we should

How do we repay the friendly smile?
The opening of a door
We can repay this with a kind word
Go on as before

We show our appreciation
Sometimes give money - yet
If we do it in a mean spirit
It does not discharge the debt

If we wish the action to continue
If we wish them to do us good
We must repay kindness with kindness
Do what we know we should

A simple smile, a wave of thanks
Will go a long way to show appreciation
We will discharge simple debts
With simple adulation

For larger measures of help
For those who do us very good
We must write a note
Or do what we can for them

35 SYSTEM ENGINEERING

System engineering is a way to work
To know how everything doth interact
You can't consider everything
That is a top level fact

System engineering has many facets
At all levels of work
If you don't take all into account
They consider you a jerk

System engineering plans our work
In each and every day
We must do the job
If we would earn our pay

System engineering we must use
The results to obtain
Sometimes seems a waste
If our minds we do not train

System engineering can be our friend
Can help us to the end
So that we can use it
Whenever a new task we begin

36 THE DENTIST

The dentist is a man of teeth
Dealing with rod and pain
Don't want to have to see him
It really is quite a bane

But when your teeth hurt
And need repair
It is a blessing indeed
To have him there

37 THE DOCTOR

Sometimes we have a hurt
A pain that will not go away
To get some relief from this
Any price we are willing to pay

We go to the doctor
In his office we sit
Then we see him
We get to say our bit

The doctor looks us over
Our temperature is taken
We hope that his digenesis
Will not be mistaken

Then we leave the office
Prescription in our hand
We get it filled at once
The pharmacist uses a generic brand

We take the medicine home
As directed we swallow the pill
No more pain
The medicine fit the bill

38 MODERN TECHNOLOGIES

Modern technologies are a boon to us
It lets us do many things
Good tidings to our work
Copious things it brings

Technologies is a fragile thing
Built one piece upon another
Pull out one tiny piece
What a pickle, oh brother

Technologies is like a house of cards
On which itself doth depend
If the foundation is pulled out
The whole will descend

39 WHAT WILL YOU DO

What will you do with your life?
With the time allotted to you
Will your life build others?
Will you be kind and just and true?

When we have left this world
Cast off this mortal coil
Our life will be judged by others
Our words, our deeds, our toil

We cannot always think of this
But we should let it guide our way
For any debts we run up
Someone will have to pay

You cannot know the end
Cannot know all things
But try, try your best to do
Those actions that kindness brings

40 WE WALK A FINE LINE

We walk a fine line
Short in time and space
From birth until death
Life travels a hectic pace

If we don't know where we're going
We don't know when we get there
If we don't set our goal
We don't have a prayer

Live life to the fullest
Keep your eye on your goal
In all things you can accomplish
Be ever bold

41 THE WORLD HAS BEEN HERE

The world has been here
For a long, long time
Our candle of life filchers and goes out
It is the Holy One's reason, rime

The future we many not know
The present is all we see
We always make our mark
To live, to love, to be

The flame of life is all we have
To build, to make, to have
It runs as long as we do fuel
But what is important is what we give

42 THE CHALLENGES WE FACE

The challenges we face
The goals we seek
Where we place our lives
Are the chains that do us keep

We can but seek the end
We seek and hope and pray
That in the end of it all
The end will be our day

To try does not mean victory
But not to try is a crime
For the goal that is our life
Will be well worth our time

43 THE RESTAURANT

You come through the door
The food to get
You look around
For a place to set

"May I help you?"
The water asks
It's my job to server
That's my task

Order the food
It's all so good
You are so hungry
Eat you would

Then it's time to leave
The service has been good
The food is what we need
We give a tip should

Let no one despise the waitress
She has done her best
For she has seen to our needs
So we can eat and rest

44 WHO IS THE EXPERT?

Who is the expert?
The one who knows
That will instill wisdom
Keep us on our toes

An expert comes from experience
From making those mistakes
Finding out the right and wrong
Finding out what it takes

We all can be experts
To those who wish to know
So that we may guide them
In the right way to go

45 WHAT A PERSON HAS

What a person has
Are what defines him here
So parting with much of them
Is more than some can bare

But things accumulate
They keep us where we are
So that we cannot move ahead
The future they do bar

There is no easy way
To part with what we have
But we must be prepared
To be able to give

46 WHEN WE WENT TO SCHOOL

When we went to school
We learned to read and write
We learned to do our numbers
But did we learn to do right?

For right and wrong
Must be taught
If we do not know the way
Our life will with error be fraught

So let us learn the lessons
Of the sage of old
When our life is judged
We will be judged as gold

47 VOLUNTEER

We often work for others
Without any pay
We wish to help out
Aid them every day

But we do it for the pay they give
It is not in money but in words true
That by their life, and by their hope
They just say "Thank you"

Thank you means so much
It really shows they care
Helps us when we sacrifice
To go and be there

48 WE WORK

We work to get things done
We may not know the end
But as we attempt the goals
We hope that we know how to begin

There are many paths to the end
We walk from day to day
If we divert our path
It will be a bad price we'll have to pay

Always keep our focus clear
Our eyes on the end goal
For it is by effort and work
That our end may be bold

There is but one way to win
Never lose our way
So that to our detractors
It will be a winning day

49 WE ARE ALL OCCUPIED

We are all occupied
Doing things all the time
Life is in the doing
Often without reason or rhyme

It is our fate
To work without stop
To do the best we can
Until we're ready to drop

But random activities
Can lead to a bad result
Can go in all directions
And get someone hurt

Thus we have managers
To give direction to what we do
But they must be directed
By someone who knows more than they knew

So work as hard as you can
Keep your spirit good
Follow the direction
Of those who know the way

50 SUCCESS

To get what you want
To want what you get
To do both
Is good, and yet

We go through life
Looking for gold
We grab at the ring
But have nothing to hold

As we work to climb
The ladder of success
To our chagrin we often find
Not happiness, but stress

So when we get
What we think we want
And it is in hand
We often find we don't

Happiness is
Wanting what we get
When it is in hand
We have the best life yet

51 AWARDS

Awards are good
They often mean a lot
Sometimes the things that are
Are not so very hot

So accept all awards
As gracefully as you can
But be careful what you say
That they don't tie your hand

52 A PROJECT

When starting a project
Whether at work or at home
The planning and preparation
Makes the end easy to hone

For planning works the problem
Before the problem works you
If you don't believe this
Try it, you'll find it is true

53 THE BUDGET PROCESS

The budget process is a bane
To all of us
When real numbers come down
Leaves us in the dust

It's nice to plan
To know what you need
But funds are limited
So have a case to plead

When the funds come for your project
Be sure that you plan to use all
For if you get funds and do not spend
The next year your plans will fall

54 BUDGET TIME

Budget time is full of fun
If the imagination doth pull
But when the funds come down
   Reality makes plans pale

Ask for what you need
Also for what you want
If you do not try and ask
When you need it you don't

55 BUDGET DAY

The sun doesn't rise
The rain doesn't go away
Everyone is yelling
Its budget day

Your future pay
Your job is on the line
You need their budget
What's yours is mine

Don't pine for money
Don't whine when stuck
Your projects not theirs
You're out of luck

56 THE MORNING GREETING

"How are you this morning?"
"How do you feel today?"
"I feel fine"
Is all I want you to say

Even if you're feeling bad
With a cold or the flue
The other person must never know
Keep it to you

The person who asked
Does not really care
He sees you and greets you
Acknowledges you're there

When you go to the doctor
The same question asked
To make you better
That is your task

So if you have bad feelings
And are dizzy or drawn
Tell those who ask
You feel just fine and run

57 BOOM YEARS

Boom years have come and gone
Destruction in their wake
If we could live them again
A different path we'd take

The oil, pools of oil
Available without end
Drove our cars, fueled our wants
Now gone, society doth rend

The air we breathe
The water we drink
Filled with chemicals
Now does it stink

The world we do hold
We live in years of boom
But ere these years do end
Our life will be gloom

There is an end to the boom
So what can we now do?
Work to save our world
Work with a way so true

We cannot save the world
From the population as a whole
But we can do our part
This will rest our soul

58 MAKE A DIFFERENCE

Make a difference
Where others have totally failed
Without putting out the effort
Human soul impelled

But we are not superior
For knowledge of the past
But must find our own way
For our knowledge to last

59 TECHNOLOGIES IS GROWING

Technologies are growing things
It coming faster all the time
Keeping up with the latest fad
Is for those in their prime

But technologies will fade
From our ever present life
Just keep and use what you need
The rest will cause much strife

60 THE INSPECTIONS

They're coming
No, they're here
Cause for trepidation
Cause for fear

When they come to the front
Open the doors wide
No place to run
No place to hide

Inspections are such a joy
They say they're here to help us
What the worry
What the fuss

We can get dinged
Our job compromised
If we do the wrong thing
If we show we despise

Inspections are a part of life
They really cause us pain
To try to cross the path
That would be insane

61 DECISIONS

Decisions are a part of life
We must forever make
They meet us at every turn
No matter what path we take

Decisions may not seem to matter
They may be insignificant and very small
But the results of how we act
May keep us from the fall

About the author

Richard Gold has been a Chrisrtian for many years and has been writing Christian poems since 2008.

He was inspired to write these poems as much of life in our civilization is concerned with the work we do to support our family and our desires.

Gold was born in Bartow Florida and has attended college and worked for the Government for 40 years. He is now retired which has given him the time necessary to produce poems among other things.

www.ingramcontent.com/pod-product-compliance
Lightning Source LLC
Chambersburg PA
CBHW060819050426
42449CB00008B/1740